JUST DAD & ME

A FATHER - SON JOURNAL

ONE·FAM

www.onefam.com

Your Family Story

Founded in 2016, OneFam is the easy way to discover, preserve and relive your family history anywhere anytime. OneFam aims to make family history available to as many families as possible. Our suite of products include Journals, Family Tree Software (web, mobile and desktop), Ancestry DNA Testing and Family History Research. Connect, share and protect your family history for generations to come.

ONE FAM

Visit us at onefam.com

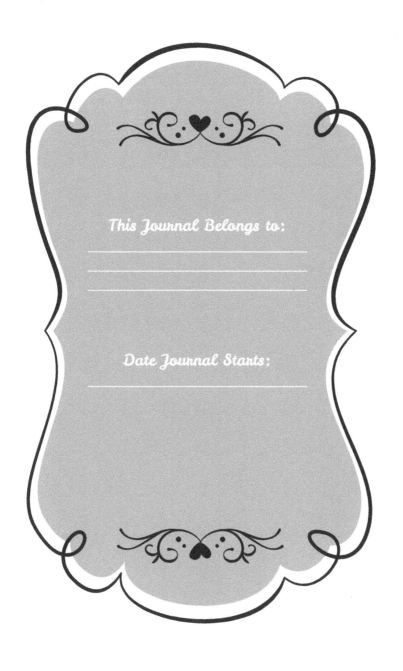

This Journal Belongs to:

_____
_____
_____

Date Journal Starts:

_____

A Father's Perspective

Your mother used to tell me that I was too hard on you, too direct, too abrupt! I always have wanted you to look at me as your super hero, your protector, your one man go-to for all of your needs. Even though it may seem that I am hard on you, it is because I want what is best for you. I want you to be strong, and fierce and able to handle whatever comes your way. I want you to be compassionate and helpful, perceptive and thoughtful.

I want you to get from me all that I did not receive from my own dad. There are so many things that I wish he had taught me…how to love, how to accept love and how to nurture those that I care for most.

Sometimes it is harder for me to find the words to tell you how much I love you. Call it machismo, call it awkwardness, you can name it whatever it is you want. Yet, it doesn't change the immense feelings of love and pride that I have for you.

I try to be a role model to you, knowing that if you see a good man, I can only hope that you will become a good man too. With everything that I do, I always remember that you are watching. I realize that you will one day follow in my footsteps rather than listen to my advice.

I want to teach you to always believe in yourself as I believe in you. You are such an amazing young man and am proud to be called your father.

I expect that you are reading this now, laughing. Laughing at dad being mushy; hysterical that dad would want to write in a journal; doubled over with laughter that your big, strong dad could possibly want to share his thoughts with you. But, the truth is, I have always wanted this…for us to share, to talk, to understand each other. I want to tell you about all the things in my life that made me who I am, including you. I want you to ask me all of the questions that you have been curious about yet too ashamed to ask.

I am sure that whatever you write in this journal, I will cry about. Yes, me! The dad who taught you to catch a football; the one who held you while they stitched your split lip; the one who gave you an "atta boy" when you went on your first date! I may not always cry like your mother or hug you like your sister, but I love you like no other.

I want this journal to be our go-to place; a safe place where you can tell me when you think I am wrong; a protected place where you feel free to share your thoughts, your emotions and your doubts. I look forward to hearing about your dreams, your aspirations and your questions.

As we move forward in this complicated world, I hope you will continue to look to me as your rock, your super hero, your super dad, using this journal as our connection to keep us moving forward…laughing and crying, together!

"When a father gives to his son, both laugh; when a son gives to his father, both cry"

~ William Shakespeare

Journal Guidelines

First and foremost, the purpose of this shared journal is…..
HAVE FUN!!! Before we begin, let's set some guidelines for sharing.

1) This should be a memorable, fun and most importantly, stress free way of sharing. If you feel it is no longer FUN and you feel it's not of benefit, perhaps it's time for a break!

2) Be Yourself! Whether you choose to share, laugh, be silly, serious, crazy, passionate or sad. Whatever makes you, YOU!

3) Who should be able to read it? This is a journal of your life, your story, ultimately you should share this with those who mean the most to you. It will strenghten your bonds and help them know more about your past, your joruney.

4) How often should we write? This can be a spur of the moment or a routine.

5) Where? How will the other one know where to read the journal? Shall we pick a "reading" place where we will pick it up?

6) Does every entry require a response? Sometimes we may just want to vent, or share, without requiring a response. How should we let the other person know that there is no need to "say" anything?

7) Have fun!!! This one is so important that it just needed to be said again.

HAPPY WRITING!

"It is not flesh and blood but the heart, which makes us fathers and sons."

Johann Schiller

"Any man can be a father but it takes someone special to be a dad."

Anne Geddes

Father Details

Name:

Nickname:

Birthday:

Star Sign:

Eye Color:

Hair Color:

Height:

Date: _____

Son Details

Name:

Nickname:

Birthday:

Star Sign:

Eye Color:

Hair Color:

Height:

Date: _____

Insert Photo

Picture of Dad

Date: _____

Insert Photo

Picture of Son

Date: _____

10 Reasons I Love My Son

1:

2:

3:

4:

5:

6:

7:

8:

9:

10:

Date: _____

10 Reasons I Love My Dad

....

....

1: ....

....

2: ....

....

3: ....

....

4: ....

....

5: ....

....

6: ....

....

7: ....

....

8: ....

....

9: ....

....

10: ....

....

....

....

....

Date: _____

★ Son

Story Time

A story about when I was a little boy: ....

....

....

....

....

....

....

....

....

....

....

....

....

....

....

....

....

....

....

....

....

Date: _____

★ Father

Story Time

A story about when I was a little boy: ....
....
....
....
....
....
....
....
....
....
....
....
....
....
....
....
....
....
....
....
....
....
....
....

Date: _____

5 Favorite Places & Why

1:

2:

3:

4:

5:

Date: _____

5 Favorite Places & Why

1: ....
....
....
....

2: ....
....
....
....

3: ....
....
....
....

4: ....
....
....
....

5: ....
....
....
....

Date: _____

Father Talk

Somethings I wish we talked about: ....

....

....

....

....

....

....

Things my father talked to me about: ....

....

....

....

....

Things I wished my father had talked to me about: ....

....

....

....

....

The first girl I had a crush on: ....

....

....

Date: _____

Son Talk

Things I would like to talk about now:
....
....
....
....
....
....
....

Things I'm not yet ready to talk about:
....
....
....
....
....

The first girl I had a crush on:
....
....
....
....
....
....
....
....
....

Date: _____

10 Favorite Songs

Father

★

Date: _____

10 Favorite Songs

Date: _____

"No love is greater than that of a father for His son."

Dan Brown

"A man knows when he is growing old because he begins to look like his father."

Gabriel Garcia Marquez

10 Favorite Books

1:

2:

3:

4:

5:

6:

7:

8:

9:

10:

Date: _____

10 Favorite Books

1:

2:

3:

4:

5:

6:

7:

8:

9:

10:

Date: _____

5 Books I Wish You Would Read

1:

2:

3:

4:

5:

Date: _____

5 Books I Wish You Would Read

1: ....
....
....
....
....

2: ....
....
....
....
....

3: ....
....
....
....
....

4: ....
....
....
....

5: ....
....
....
....

Date: _____

Drawing of the Happiest Day

Draw a picture of the happiest day you remember.

Date: _____

Drawing of the Happiest Day

Draw a picture of the happiest day you remember.

Date: _____

Insert Photo

A picture of us doing something
we love together.

Date: _____

Insert Photo

A picture of us doing something
we love together.

Date: _____

Tell Me a Story

About: ....

....

Story: ....

....

....

....

....

....

....

....

....

....

....

....

....

....

....

....

....

Father

Date: _____

Tell Me a Story

About: ....

....

Story: ....

....

....

....

....

....

....

....

....

....

....

....

....

....

....

....

....

....

....

....

....

....

....

Date: _____

Son

Childhood Memories

A description of how life was growing up as a child:

Date: _____

Childhood Memories

A description of how life was growing up as a child:

....

....

....

....

....

....

....

....

....

....

....

....

....

....

....

....

....

....

....

....

Date: _____

My 5 Best Friends & Why

1:

2:

3:

4:

5:

Date: _____

My 5 Best Friends & Why

1: ....

....

....

....

2: ....

....

....

....

3: ....

....

....

....

4: ....

....

....

....

5: ....

....

....

....

Date: _____

★ Son

What causes problems between us:

How I act when I'm annoyed or angry with you:

How I wish you would respond:

How I could respond better:

Date: _____

Feelings & Emotions

What causes problems between us:
....

....

....

....

....

How I act when I'm annoyed or angry with you:
....

....

....

....

....

How I wish you would respond:
....

....

....

....

....

How I could respond better:
....

....

....

....

....

Date: _____

Feelings & Emotions

How I feel during an argument:

How I feel after an argument:

How I try to fix things afterwards:

Date: _____

Feelings & Emotions

How I feel during an argument:

....

....

....

....

....

....

How I feel after an argument:

....

....

....

....

....

....

How I try to fix things afterwards:

....

....

....

....

....

....

Date: _____

Son

Father

Date: _____

Son's Notes

....
....
....
....
....
....
....
....
....
....
....
....
....
....
....
....
....
....
....
....
....
....
....

Date: _____

Father

Date: _____

Remember That Time....

....
....
....
....
....
....
....
....
....
....
....
....
....
....
....
....
....
....
....
....
....
....
....
....

Son

Date: _____

Things to Do Together - Bucket List

Father

1:

2:

3:

4:

5:

6:

7:

8:

9:

10:

Date:

Things to Do Together - Bucket List

....

....

1: ....

2: ....

3: ....

4: ....

5: ....

6: ....

7: ....

8: ....

9: ....

10: ....

....

....

....

....

Date: _____

Son

About:

Story:

Father

Date: _____

Tell Me a Story

About:
....

....

Story:
....

....

....

....

....

....

....

....

....

....

....

....

....

....

....

....

....

....

....

....

....

Date: _____

Son

My 5 Earliest Childhood Memories

Father

1: ....
....
....
....

2: ....
....
....
....

3: ....
....
....
....

4: ....
....
....
....

5: ....
....
....
....

Date: _____

My 5 Earliest Childhood Memories

1: ....
....
....
....
....

2: ....
....
....
....
....

3: ....
....
....
....
....

4: ....
....
....
....
....

5: ....
....
....
....
....

Date: _____

Son ★

Insert Photo

Find a photo from
your childhood.

Date: _____

Insert Photo

Find a photo from

your childhood.

Date: _____

Things You Don't Know About Me

1:

2:

3:

4:

5:

6:

7:

8:

9:

10:

Date: _____

Things You Don't Know About Me

1:

2:

3:

4:

5:

6:

7:

8:

9:

10:

Date: _____

Dreams & Goals

What I wanted to be growing up: ....

....

....

....

Jobs I worked in and why: ....

....

....

....

....

....

....

....

What I would like for my son in 5 years: ....

....

....

....

....

....

....

....

Date: _____

Dreams & Goals

What I wanted to be growing up:
....
....
....
....

Jobs I would like to have in the future:
....
....
....
....
....
....
....
....

What I would like for my father in 5 years:
....
....
....
....
....
....
....

Date: _____

Father

Where I would like to be in 5 years:

Where I would like to be in 10 years:

What I wish I had done 10 years ago:

Date:

Dreams & Goals

Where I would like to be in 5 years: ....
....
....
....
....
....
....
....

Where I would like to be in 10 years: ....
....
....
....
....
....
....
....

Where I would like to be in 15 years: ....
....
....
....
....
....
....

Date: _____

Drawing of Life in the Future

Draw a picture of the world in 100 years time.

Date: _____

Drawing of Life in the Future

Draw a picture of the world in 100 years time.

Date: _____

"There must always be a struggle between a father and son, while one aims at power and the other at independence."

Samuel Johnson

"My father gave me the greatest gift anyone could give another person, he believed in me."

Jim Valvano

My Greatest Accomplishments

1:

2:

3:

4:

5:

6:

7:

8:

9:

10:

Date: _____

My Greatest Accomplishments

1:

2:

3:

4:

5:

6:

7:

8:

9:

10:

Date: _____

Father

Details of my education:

....
....
....
....
....

How I feel about my education:

....
....
....
....
....

What I wish I had done differently:

....
....
....
....
....
....

Things I would like to help you with:

....
....
....
....

Date: _____

Education

Why do you think education is important:

....

....

....

....

How do you feel about your grades:

....

....

....

....

What you can do to improve:

....

....

....

....

Things you would like more help with:

....

....

....

....

Date: _____

Insert Photo

A picture of your first day at
school or college.

Date: _____

Insert Photo

A picture of your first day at school or college.

Date: _____

Times You Made Me Proud

1: ....
....
....
....

2: ....
....
....
....

3: ....
....
....
....

4: ....
....
....
....

5: ....
....
....
....

Father

Date: _____

Times You Made Me Proud

1: ....
....
....
....

2: ....
....
....
....

3: ....
....
....
....

4: ....
....
....
....

5: ....
....
....
....

Date: _____

★ Son

How Do You Know I Love You

Draw/illustrate or write the things that show your love.

Date: _____

How Do You Know I Love You

Draw/illustrate or write the things that show your love.

Date: _____

Tell Me a Story

About:

Story:

Father

Date:

Tell Me a Story

About: ....

....

Story: ....

....

....

....

....

....

....

....

....

....

....

....

....

....

....

....

....

....

....

....

....

....

....

Date: _____

My Biggest Regrets in Life

Father

1:

2:

3:

4:

5:

What I have learned from my regrets:

Date: _____

My Biggest Regrets in Life

1: ....

....

....

....

2: ....

....

....

....

3: ....

....

....

....

4: ....

....

....

....

5: ....

....

....

....

What I have learned from my regrets: ....

....

....

....

....

Date: _____

Insert Photo

My Favorite Photo of
us together

Date: _____

Insert Photo

My Favorite Photo of

us together

Date: _____

Father's Notes

Date: _____

Son's Notes

Date: _____

10 Things I Love

1:

2:

3:

4:

5:

6:

7:

8:

9:

10:

Date: _____

10 Things I Love

1: ....

2: ....

3: ....

4: ....

5: ....

6: ....

7: ....

8: ....

9: ....

10: ....

Date: _____

★ Son

10 Things I Hate

1:

2:

3:

4:

5:

6:

7:

8:

9:

10:

Date: _____

10 Things I Hate

1: ....

2: ....

3: ....

4: ....

5: ....

6: ....

7: ....

8: ....

9: ....

10: ....

Date: _____

Remember That Time.....

Father

Date: _____

Remember That Time....

Date: _____

If I Had 3 Wishes

1:

2:

3:

Date: _____

If I had 3 Wishes

1:
....
....
....
....
....
....
....
....

2:
....
....
....
....
....
....

3:
....
....
....
....
....
....

Date: _____

★ Son

"A father is a man who expects his son to be as good a man as he meant to be."

Frank A. Clark

"It's a father's duty to give his sons a fine chance."

George Eliot

Tell Me a Story

About: ....

Story: ....

....

....

....

....

....

....

....

....

....

....

....

....

....

....

....

....

....

....

....

Father

⭐

Date: _____

Tell Me a Story

About: ....

....

Story: ....

....

....

....

....

....

....

....

....

....

....

....

....

....

....

....

....

....

....

....

....

....

....

Date: _____

Draw a picture of an item, object or place you like.

Date: _____

Drawing of Something I Like

Draw a picture of an item, object or place you like.

Date: _____

Father

Why We are Different

Date: _____

Why We are the Same

....
....
....
....
....
....
....
....
....
....
....

Why We are Different

....
....
....
....
....
....
....
....
....
....

Date: _____

Describe Your Son

Date: _____

Describe Your Father

Date: _____

Funny Things You Have Said or Done

Date: _____

Funny Things You Have Said or Done

....
....
....
....
....
....
....
....
....
....
....
....
....
....
....
....
....
....
....
....
....
....
....
....

Son

Date: _____

Father

What is your favorite color?

....

....

What is your shoe size?

....

....

....

What city were you born in?

....

....

What is your favorite dessert and why?

....

....

....

....

What is your favorite movie & why?

....

....

....

....

What is your favorite TV series and why?

....

....

....

....

Date: _____

Quick Questions

What is your favorite color?

....

....

What is your shoe size?

....

....

....

What city were you born in?

....

....

What is your favorite dessert and why?

....

....

....

....

What is your favorite movie & why?

....

....

....

....

What is your favorite TV series and why?

....

....

....

....

....

Date: _____

Father

If you could visit any place in the world, where would it be and why?

....
....
....
....
....
....

If you could travel back in time to one moment, what would that moment be and why?

....
....
....
....

What is your favorite sport or hobby?

....
....
....
....

What is your favorite season?

....

Date: _____

Quick Questions

If you could visit any place in the world, where would it be and why?

....

....

....

....

....

....

If you could change anything about your life, what would it be?

....

....

....

....

....

What is your favorite sport or hobby?

....

....

....

....

What is your favorite season?

....

Date: _____

Drawing of A Memory

Draw a picture of a memory you cherish.

Drawing of A Memory

Draw a picture of a memory you cherish.

Date: _____

5 Best Things About You

1:

2:

3:

4:

5:

Date: _____

5 Best Things About You

1: ....
....
....
....
....

2: ....
....
....
....
....

3: ....
....
....
....
....

4: ....
....
....
....

5: ....
....
....
....
....

Date: _____

Son

5 Things You Do That Annoy Me

Father

1:
....
....
....
....

2:
....
....
....
....
....

3:
....
....
....
....

4:
....
....
....
....

5:
....
....
....
....

Date: _____

5 Things You Do That Annoy Me

1: ....
....
....
....

2: ....
....
....
....

3: ....
....
....
....

4: ....
....
....

5: ....
....
....
....

Date: _____

Son

Recipe for favorite Food We Make

Write down the recipe for your favorite food.

Father

Date: _____

Recipe for Favorite Food We Make

Write down the recipe for your favorite food.

....

....

....

....

....

....

....

....

....

....

....

....

....

....

....

....

....

....

....

....

....

....

Date: _____

About:

....

....

Story:

....

....

....

....

....

....

....

....

....

....

....

....

....

....

....

....

....

....

....

....

....

....

Father

Date: _____

Tell Me a Story

About:
....

....

Story:
....

....

....

....

....

....

....

....

....

....

....

....

....

....

....

....

....

....

....

....

....

Date: _____

Family Holidays

Write the details of your family holidays, the locations and favorite father/son memories from the holiday.

Date: _____

Family Holidays

Write the details of your family holidays, the locations and favorite father/son memories from the holiday.

....

....

....

....

....

....

....

....

....

....

....

....

....

....

....

....

....

....

....

....

....

....

Date: _____

Insert Photo

A picture of us on a

family holiday

Date: _____

Insert Photo

A picture of us on a
family holiday

Date: _____

"The father who does not teach his son his duties is equally guilty with the son who neglects them."

Ralph Waldo Emerson

"By the time a man realizes that maybe his father was right, he usually has a son who thinks he's wrong."

Charles Wadsworth

Father

Date: _____

Remember That Time....

....
....
....
....
....
....
....
....
....
....
....
....
....
....
....
....
....
....
....
....
....
....
....
....
....

Date: _____

Insert Photo

Photos of us at the same age

Date: _____

Insert Photo

Photos of us at the same age

Date: _____

What sports and hobbies interest you?

Would you like to share any of the above with your son?

Date: _____

Sports & Hobbies

What sports and hobbies interest you?

....
....
....
....
....
....
....
....
....
....
....
....
....

Would you like to share any of the above with your father?

....
....
....
....
....
....
....
....

Date: _____

What Did You Learn from this Journal

Date: _____

What Did You Learn from this Journal

Date: _____

Father's Notes

Date: _____

Son's Notes

Date: _____

Father

Date: _____

Son's Notes

Date: _____

Date: _____

Son's Notes

Date: _____

Father's Notes

Date: _____

Son's Notes

....

....

....

....

....

....

....

....

....

....

....

....

....

....

....

....

....

....

....

....

....

....

Date: _____

Father

Date: _____

Son's Notes

Son

Date: _____

Sign Up to OneFam

At OneFam we aim to make family history available to everyone. We would like to invite you to become a member of OneFam community and enjoy exclusive benefits. With already over 25,000 users worldwide, we promise you'll be in good company.

- **50%** off your next journal purchases
- **A**ccess to free family tree software
- **B**irthday gifts
- **F**ree shipping offers
- **F**irst dibs on sales
- **&** more...

To subscribe, simply visit our website at:

https://www.onefam.com/subscribe/

ONE FAM

Create Your Family Free

Get started with your free online family tree in minutes. Simply sign up, add your parents, siblings, children, grandparents and other family members.

- Preserve Images, Videos, Audio, Stories & Events
- Invite & Connect with Family Members
- Create and Share Family History
- Available on Web, Mobile and Ipad

ONE FAM

www.onefam.com

More Great Journals

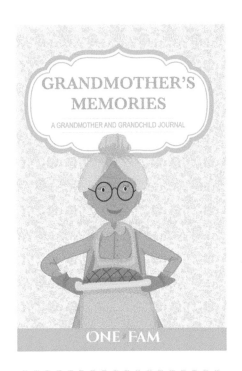

GRANDMOTHER'S MEMORIES

A GRANDMOTHER AND GRANDCHILD JOURNAL

ONE FAM

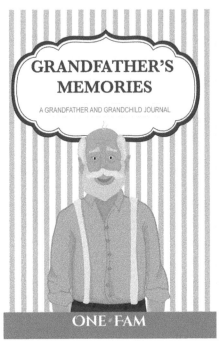

GRANDFATHER'S MEMORIES

A GRANDFATHER AND GRANDCHILD JOURNAL

ONE FAM

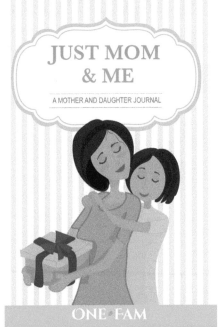

JUST MOM & ME

A MOTHER AND DAUGHTER JOURNAL

ONE FAM

JUST MOM & ME

A MOTHER AND SON JOURNAL

ONE FAM

Visit Onefam.com for our full range

More Great Journals

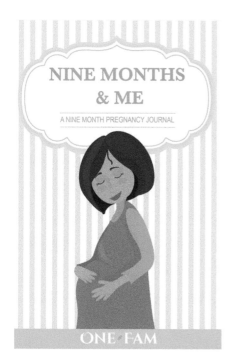

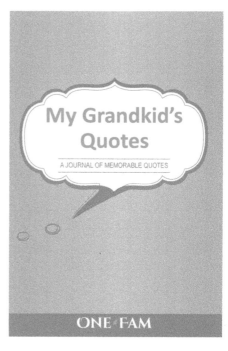

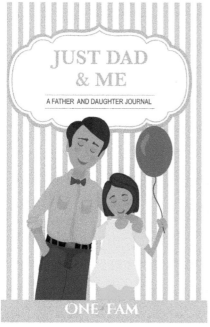

Visit Onefam.com for our full range